# MILES PRESS

Indiana University South Bend Department of English

# PRECARIOUS

42 Miles Press
Editor, David Dodd Lee
Copyright© 2014 Allan Peterson.  All rights reserved.
ISBN  978-0-9830747-4-8 (pbk. alk. paper)

For permission, required to reprint or broadcast more than several lines, write to:
42 Miles Press, Department of English, Indiana University South Bend
1700 Mishawaka Avenue, South Bend, IN 46615

http://42milespress.com

Art Direction, Nick Kuder, Design, John-Mark Cuarto, Production, Paul Sizer
The Design Center, Frostic School Of Art, Western Michigan University.
Printing, McNaughton & Gunn, Inc.

# PRECARIOUS

# POEMS
# BY
# ALLAN
# PETERSON

# CONTENTS

Acknowledgments

Terrible things began with me

in the midst of radio and lightning

People said such things had been going on

for some time but I had no proof

O there were books and pictures

and children had been poisoned

by whistles made from the stems

of cow parsnip and there were sad songs

and the sounds of bombing

but I thought that was because there was never

a time when we weren't dreaming

I remember it must have been windier then

Snow swirled around houses

under an apparent bowl of stars

There were paperweights everywhere

## REMINDERS

Who speaks for the body? We do.

Every eminence named, each fossa,

eloquent structures of shining bones

as if standing undone on a hill above Urbino,

artists making bright lines in bright sun,

bright language as the bones resurface

after an interim of flesh. Ribs, phalanges,

wings of the sphenoid, shapes named

for what they resemble, scapula a spade.

And how we look lovingly seeing a body

that does not clatter apart, that articulates

without ligaments, that presents in October

poignant reminders begging at our doors.

## PRECARIOUS

Winds and the half-winds and half that charted.

Heart and the half-hearted notched and noticed.

Still it's precarious to set out from Carthage

with just love and a lodestone, wet rope for ballast.

If the stutterer sings, it's smooth sailing.

If the whistler sits in the bowsprit, there's trouble.

The sentence will not complete, nor the voyage.

Always something more, another noun.

Now songbirds find the owl and scold the oaks.

Imagine the terror of jaws before the compass,

shoals as the premeditated curseworks of heaven.

## LIKE AFFECTION

Hands clutched to a throat is a predicament

a body taken suddenly with the threat of survival

an entire understanding of the urgency of time

and need for five blows with the heel of a hand

between shoulder blades

Normal so called could be a day when sparrows

build a nest in the gutter or someone swallows

a button battery and instead of reaching for a broom

you wrap your arms around them like affection

but backwards bending them slightly forward

so they cannot see the nest give them a quick

upward thrust repeated if needed and sparrows

will exit the downspout

## THE USUAL HORSES

One thing entry to another:

a death cake protecting a corpse viewing,

ocean going emerald to ash

saying preciousness is change:

the picture taken too soon from developers

so that persons expected do not appear:

loon that took the bait by mistake

taking Jason a hundred yards

from a man hunting dinner to a boat

harnessed to a bird:

the usual horses grazing back in the yard,

brass dogs still holding the door.

## EVENLY US

The brain has a sense of itself

the mind, and the mind

has a sense of itself, the soul

and the soul sees itself

in others as if a single being.

That's how we see it.

The owners having been briefed,

who present to each other

a resumé of dreams as credentials

and the bones in a jar named for us.

Us evenly, us symmetrical,

us with our charming illusions,

saying from the heart, your breathing

is mine, and meaning it.

## CENTURIES TO QUIT

The last person we know that smokes is retiring

and so ending two long habits: quitting and not quitting

which battled with each other. In the paradox of the old

making the next civilization out of its newspapers,

his most beautiful city has been ruined by shelling.

Black clouds drift above Dubrovnik. No one changes

when angry or hungry, and it may take Africa and Europe

centuries to quit making Asia seem habit forming.

It is as poignant as the last of the elephants

eating the last of the trees at Tsavo because we made them,

and made religion, and nations that made them sacred,

turned them out of paradise for more farmland. We can't stop

thinking we're more important, and they cannot forget

the earth can be fully digested with its thorns.

That a man can look into his x-rays for shadows in Latin

and find enough fluid in his joints to put out his cigarette.

When it's finally too late, the few remaining people on TV

are sawing all the trees out of Sarajevo to burn after furniture

is gone, after history is coldly unconvinced by its future.

## ALL THIS INSTEAD

He wanted it special so he planned on releasing

a dozen white doves sent from Connecticut

after reading the passage from Psalms

and the words especially written by his cousin

the poet composed he said as if music itself.

And the rows of oak so the sound deflected

and combined above the audience in a way

fractal like the galaxy and the same was true

above the ushers wearing gloves with a button

at the place where the *palmaris longus* meets

and feathers into the *flexor retinaculum*.

All this instead of just stepping into the garden

as it was where one *vanessa* might be nectaring a rose.

## CONTINENTAL

We were sinking

The windows were filling with cities

as if poured into glasses

No one was thinking of drowning

No one thinking air ship

but there we were submerging

A captain turned off the cabin lights

We folded our tables   heading down quietly

The moon holding its breath floated up

## EASY BELIEVERS

Last night tried to accentuate the stars

by staying darker than usual

the dark of the body inside the body

onyx as Satan's crows

suggesting it had been touched in places

with a hot wire like a skin

that powders from that same experience

We are easy believers

and it takes only some voice of authority

to say inside the body

is none of our business if organs shift positions

at night and a cure is to drink

nettle from a church bell   or that to survive curses

a mandrake must be uprooted

by a black dog on a rope then struck dead

## TRANSIT

We live by a warm sea glittering with moons

having the power to hog beauty for themselves

the way Hubble is the archangel announcing

more births than we can manage and wind

bringing out thousands of white gloves

for such occasions   my moon app showing me

thin phases daily   loading the vast black first

then luxury passes   cabin cruisers with music

waving and streaming back in lost scarves

## FULL

In the kitchen with linoleum and glass,

an enameled sink and steel

refrigerator or the other way around,

we could hear almost nothing

of Terry's urgent rendition of St. Luke.

The ceramic platters, the stainless,

nothing to stick to, everyone talking at once,

a secular thunder loose

in the kitchen, sound bouncing like lasers

from mirrors till nothing

more could fit, not another physicist, not

the reflective evangelist, not

the spirits of the clanging and biblical dead.

## SECOND OPINION

Used or ignored the dictionary retains its power like the plastic skull

that glowed on my keychain at night powered by the diagrams

and paragraphs of everything from aleph, our grinning bones, to ship knots,

a lexicon of leaves: lanceolate, ovate, palmate, and explaining the difference

between some stone-colored dove at Wakulla and another pigeon drinking

through its nostrils in a continuous stream to the final zed for lightning.

I've added *Amphineura*, the knuckle chitons, by being there in the curative

nature-as-pages, added fern floors in Washington and clastic rocks,

Gunnison's green aspens holding the 45 degree sky weft with its migrating spiders,

added the moon that barked out two clouds over Lake Quinault like speech,

added the anthracite jetties well before sunrise to the Pacific at La Push

where the Quileute practiced their canoes for the race to Bella Bella,

a singer's arms beckoning in as the words *love's hard luck*, like the rivers

going out fully dressed, the radio, the air above it that uncurled like questions.

## OPEN TO BOWSTRING

There are the phoebes, here hospice,

chamfron protecting the forehead of a horse

engraved on mild steel with roses.

With enough attention a logic assembles,

as when opening to "bowstring"

I sense tension, then the yew shaft's feather.

I turn to "target" by coincidence;

there is no escaping one's complicity in chance.

Then I open to "battlement," then "fletcher."

## KNOWLEDGE FIRST

We call it knowledge first to be nice, then superstition

if it's theirs, then demonic if it means contradiction.

Remember the Tree of it, how dangerous, how nothing stays

in its place once you know feathers drop symmetrically

so the skimmer doesn't fly in a circle. The very idea

of *its place* is the forcing of facts into a philosophy

someone is paying to maintain. The moment the sugar

crystals surrender to syrup out of sheer curiosity

they start to rebuild again drying to a small city on the knife.

Lilacs are massaged along the fence by windy hands.

You can see them give and moan from their fingers.

This is what they told us we'd die from, wasn't it

—love, teeth first in the pinnate leaves, then the hickory

chewing on its lip lies to us again. How after dying it recants.

## A PRIORI

I felt it, my femur, one end of the classic

cartoon dogbone where it fits my hip

same as inside the legs of the marble figures

in Piazza Navona who were rivers as people

its condyle sometimes a rueful fist

shaking a little if I overflex on leg-presses

remindful of the great sculptural regret

that we will not continue to happen

long enough or be the perfectly boneless

spirits that dance water through themselves

**REWRITE**

Which words to marshal and which to let go

because they will be back?

Just these this time, so mouths would move seeing them

and the killdeer on one leg would be there,

if that's what it was, or the kiss in its stirring, or the mouse

or fish crows black as the priests of Boston.

And the voice in the mind would say them faithfully,

the quality of storm mentioned again creating low pressure,

hairs standing up on your forearm

like signals from wavelets to the agitated leaves of hickory

even in the middle of Books-A-Million.

## SAY SPARINGLY

I haven't got time for fiction and its assumption

that someone has that many hours just to sit around

only to arrive after so many pages at such limited conclusions.

I have daymares to deal with after all. Urgencies. My sweater

itself a single yarn crimped like secret script into a dense message.

I spark touching the door.   All I need is to say sparingly

leave gaping spaces the opposite of Inca stones for elephants

of meaning to slip in with their silvery knife blades.

Everyone already comes prepared with details and descriptions.

I need not provide an album and dictionary   a history

with labeled china and leaves stuck on   nights and named lovers

on their arms.   Just a room in which rivers meet a tree

with birds for leaves growing through the roof

from the floral upholstery   a vista back and forward

to be put on like long gloves   a pearl upstairs for light

shaded by Levalours and a hush of paint.

## HEAT ESCAPING THROUGH MY HEAD

Granite remembers fire like Gulf sand

the mountains of Carolina

*Ilex* leaf shadows on weathered wood grain

reconstruct fragments

of a Qashq'ai rug so that this remembrance

might drift in

below the angel's warm garden o's woven

that the calories

might escape like a lace scarf

But freezing now

the stiff plants have turned to lettuce my heart

sticks close recalling

thoughts of the tram that cannot leave its wire

## SUCH THINGS

The shastas are chest high and yet to bloom

but move to the sun with their eyes closed

I hear the cottonwoods open their hymnals

Because of such things the voice in my hand

speaks to paper   I am that close to shadowless

I love through the window through layers

of clothing into the photograph   I see the life

to come is tomorrow   finches turning gold

garlic on its long stalk inclined and split

## DON'T FORGET US

Autotomy in spiders is a voluntary act.

With such surprises, anticipation should have them

humming like the truck of wear-dated carpet

that idled all night in the Hardee's parking lot.

Yesterday at the falls above the old quarry

a man put a running shoe on his plastic leg

for a fleet and normal look the way poetry evokes things

only potentially there, things attached for survival.

Then what was taken from the cliff became a lake

bathers spun down to on a single string.

What comes after is unknown, how a spider throws a leg,

us leaving our pennies where they fall.

What could it cost the present if a few heads were missing,

discovered eventually black as frostbite,

meaning don't forget us, we are leaving things behind.

## YOU HELPLESS

The holly dentate, the bald elm grimacing,

ragged threats and toothed smiles by thousands,

delicate boxwoods trimmed into animals.

Seeing them at sundown you'd think

the hills were on fire and the wildlife had gathered

to ask for protection, for help overcoming

their stationary fear of such blazing vermilions.

Then you look down and see your shoes

making hooves of your feet, stamping and anxious

as one of them with a bad ear, a good side.

# I SPEAK TO THE HOUSE ABOUT WATER

It tells me rock scissors roof

that seepage has patterns

we cannot anticipate

that leaves clogging gutters

fall by abscission and clouds

are the ghosts of moisture


It shows me light blinding its windows

and night waiting a turn on the wet trunks

Now the house is whispering

about the sounds of paving one street over


I'll tell you what I know about the house

If I tell it how my hand can fly

out the window of a car banking the wind

it will keep me warm after sundown

It is crazy for stories of things that move

## FEELING LIKE THE AFRICAN

Where I am, with me is

Frances to whom my muscles are attached,

dogs that perk with a whistle,

catching urgency from whatever state I call.

Even the strangest will do the same:

And what has flown low below me, stingrays,

loons, hooded mergansers

the almost frozen wolf eel ribboned in the depths,

whose beauty is my god's

revenge on austerity, whose cloudy wrist tells time,

white as a moonstone.

But I have no god.   It is just me feeling like the African

figure full of nails

that says the future is likely all rust and worms, muscular,

attentive, but with extra dogs.

## EVERY DAY

Every day if not sooner or more often

I find a small surprise

Today a scorpion that overwintered in the latch

bird on the roof peak

like a prow and the house sailing faster therefore

to bring both of us and guano and oak leaves

closer to the coast where I am

turning the fish skull so the sun can bleach it

to go inside with the ormolu spoons

helmet shells and other treasures of the beauty

of death in life

## EQUINOX

The world is the large body next to me

It has the right to remain silent but does not

We exchange breaths

At night we wear the same color

and pass through each other without being noticed

What I forget about is there

Our footprints are filling with pictures of water

Streets are being doubled by wet lights

The months of visible breaths are beginning

## BEGINNING AGAIN

There is a door that closes April

and opens May

It is paper and its numbers remember nothing

after thirty-one


Things begin again the way I can enter one room

and forget another

like a past life where the water has boiled away


In fifteen eighty-two ten days

were removed from the calendar causing riots

for wages and lost birthdays


and today the day shortened an hour

and I became president

once again of the room behind the door


The ghosts pass again before the porch

the cruelest door

The riots continue now but more faintly

## SECOND SIGHT

No soul. No gods. No hidden sun behind the one we have. No other world adrift

in the hall mirror. No money back on the death offer. She said sometimes a baby

is born with a caul. A skin veil. A sign of second sight. That the common is not

alike each time and is therefore misnamed. The exceptions are numinous.

A child special-delivered with an onion skin letter from the shivering molecules.

A deep see-through angel. Meaning things arrive without asking. You just guess

and suppose until something answers back unexpectedly and you tell a friend

excitedly how it had wings and appeared right in the middle of the shopping center

with gauze for clouds and its own photographer. Look at what we take for normal.

The desire is so deep to be and be assured we are something other than we are

as when palm trees are fireworks but so slow we take them for botany.   She smiles.

Teeth behind her lips show light can originate from inside the body along with the Dark

Ages that happen every night. We can lie down anywhere. On the grass. The dock.   Over

each other and look below us into the microscope. First there is nothing

till we learn how. Then everything moves and jostles. We want to tell someone

as if we were Cortez. Shout. Write home. Sing our way to the unexplored interior.

Remember forever since we can't predict. Life is continuous from atoms to email.

More at both ends. We lament our crude tools. Words. Fever. An old Smith-Corona

with manual return. A machine forgotten like the old days when it was common to write

heavens with a goose feather as someone in the pageant with fake wings reminds us.

## AS FAR AS I KNOW

As far as I know is not that far

I step outside to visit my mosquitoes

A boat winch strains to be a voice

There is no memory without remorse

The slightest passing thought

says poignant on the way

and poignant has a voice like that

a cry   a winch lifting daylight and daylight

dropped from a great height

## BEFORE IT'S OVER

One cannot study history fast enough or imagine,

so much is missing faster than before.

So I want to take Frances to Ozette to count mosses,

the zigzag joints of salal

tacking to the coast before it's over, the old life,

see elk wheezing and bellowing

while there are some, remind children and visitors

the razor clam was named

for a look-alike steel blade they've never seen

folded for safety in its case,

a fibula, like a forearm touched back to its shoulder.

## THE INEVITABLE

To have that letter arrive

was like the mist that took a meadow

and revealed hundreds

of small webs once invisible

The inevitable often

stands by plainly but unnoticed

till it hands you a letter

that says death and you notice

the weed field had been

readying its many damp handkerchiefs

all along

## I AM MISSING

I am missing a sense of the spins and rotations

in all but the simplest applications

where the shadows cast by planets should fall

across a moon like black flashlights

I can accommodate to dancing with its goofy loops

but am baffled how a man who earlier

had peeled skin from a captive or eaten his heart

would know what day there will be no shadows

in the doorway of Temple 22 at Copán

## MY OWN RECOGNIZANCE

Trees blown out of the yards leave only flowers
like bows from lost shoes and their ominous heel-holes

The moon and moon snails have traded places
Trucks are trying to harmonize on the last passable road

If I am called on to explain the recognition of being
ultimately alone I say it is like the building catching fire

You are trying to escape with the rest and your sleeve
is snatched by a doorknob   You are yanked backwards

How disturbing the breaks in expected regularity
picket gaps pines   torqued to splinters   the mystery

of who lets off steam in a whistle that carries a mile
the repeatable joy of a tree frog housed in a broom handle

or taking a clock apart and staring at the impossibility
of reassembly   or trying to recreate a chair

with meteors in its wood and amber needles like a school
of minnows   First things first but easier said than sorted

First the blisters then leather relaxes forgetting it was skin
And longitude and lassitude how do they survive

How does the dateline work   How far west of recovery
does the arbitrary start   How thin the appearances we trust

We think we can stand in the present and reconstruct the past
from leftovers but look what is happening to Phoenix

on weather radar how braid and ribbon come together
like bees and wind at the entrance of a flower

I have been pleased to discover the concept of nothing
is only predicted by the body of the universe but not required

More likely is abundance More to the point is the mythical
the little left to explain embodied in the common no less

than in the burning of elements in the interior of stars
and the certainty of thrill when Frances whose real name

I have yet to learn comes out of the bedroom wearing
only the silver necklace from Afghanistan

## THE SPACES

As you are taught in drawing the spaces

between things are equally substance

Intimate distances are a thing's identifier

The arm is corrected by the shape between

the model's body and the silver compote

There are the usual leaves in the window

They make the birds think they can fly

through the dining room from the space

between the house and flagstone   It's how

the cascade skippers find the lavender

and inquisitive dust finds the light shafts

## ENTRANCE

If I go to this side   the nesting wrens frenzy

on the other   thorns turn on me like migraines

To the right the blistering siding

left   the precipitous ditch

Between them a broken flagstone

whose crack could be an entrance

to the underworld   *is* an entrance

to the underworld   but so are the post holes

and the wellhead

I enter   I am welcomed by the emissary mole

and the rich aroma of free will and worms

I move a stone and see the curled grub

that must be that to be the beautiful beetle

and over me the hawk whose short wings fit

between trees   examines the hot grasses

whose lives are brush strokes hiding field mice

## HARD TIMES

Thanksgiving and transient asters

of north wind bloom on aluminum

as sea gulls plunder mergansers

I had been watching accidentals

and the wood that turns liquid

and the anxious copper-covered wren

Machinery is no metaphor for this

nor scapula nor a trace of chains

In hard times we simply acknowledge

each relentless hour has sixty teeth

## A SIMPLE THING

Sometimes they will come

as if just born from the dark

between the houses or out of the opposite

of dissolve under the apple

from fog that sleeps in the fields at night

I look up from this line and a doe

is standing before me an empty space

only two words ago

It is a simple thing to lose the universe

an eyelid will do

## WHETHER NEITHER

Whether neither in the sentence

is singular or plural

Whether heartbreak in Alabama

is one or too many

as often as the moons of Jupiter

Whether grey as yesterday is Paine's

or charcoal or the rest of Isadore

now inland and dissipating

Whether ardor is an instant or a list

Whether breath is wasted

sober cold   rich are idle

Whether knowing all along is all

## PROOF

As if to prove the immensity and certainty of something unbelievable

were three pages of zeros single-spaced preceded by a one a light year

of dollars Isn't that the size of a national economy three trillion

of them the number of cells in the average body human I mean

Isn't it also the number of cars on global roads that put end to end

would go X times to the moon and back or equal the weight

of springtails and grubs under an acre of anywhere in Iowa

Doesn't it mean hydrogen is as heavy in its atoms as the earth

and its ocean the charge of an electron somehow more than lightning

more than whatever demonstrated bomb we use to measure real power

splitting the dark from what we know is comfort from enemies

and from which black nothing nothing escapes. But most convincing

is when in a darkened room they start the home movies on the old Bell

& Howell and you hold up your arm palm open and out of the light

the dust in the air containing a few molecules we're told of everything

that ever existed the way that from a thimble full of Thames a little

will be in Montpelier the children from years ago yourself included

start sledding on your hand.

## NOW AND THEN

Winter revisits through the white rose

and a crow makes the sound of last year's

boat winch Everything is something else

for the moment   Even the wind

with its rasp tongue relents now and then

and the names of the recent dead gather

on the freezing granite

Still we sing and recite

No sense wasting a good grief

## FEAR OF FIRE

Within the fear of fire was the fear horses would burn

in those scenes with the barn ablaze and they couldn't save them.

The ocean is fireproof. Any wave below me could smother

the smallest spark, help bells ready to dong in the channel.

No horses, no running, nothing with long legs to be seen.

Then I hear diesels and hoofbeats. Something is going up

over the horizon in a big way, the wind moving to see it

taking the buoy's long warnings. Then footprints start on water

from the offshore breeze. Cloud smoke layers at the edge

of the shadow of the fear of everything in sight catching

and each diesel leaving the slips in this early light is a fireboat.

I see yesterday burns up and today is burning down,

that everyday fear runs from the actual, each morning a fire drill,

each boat a rescue. Each piston escaping hoofbeats on a bridge.

## BURN

He said the steam comes out star-shaped

You have to be careful when frothing soy

and talking to a customer like a letter to the editor

holding your hand to avoid scalding

the part star shape plays in exuberance and danger

what is stellar and what is palmate

ways they come together milk thistle with thorns

cappuccino piping hot with a flower in the foam

## FLORIDA

We had been wondering what signs to trust

No Life Guard on Duty or the skin deep trees

already shivering on the surface of the pool

The first shadows were condos palms

a dozen gulls bright as tusks

It was just another day of someone running

those puffy clouds past the post card hotels

sea grape leaves like dinner plates an illusion

of real life maintained by sweating machinery

## TRAVELOGUE

In my system molecules call the radio to order

and I am counting how full the air is of pollen

mold and the husks of spiders hiding in the broom

thinking how the lamp at home was turned to an acorn

stained walnut cap crisscrossed with cuts for realism

how folding the map weakens it and after the first crease

nothing restores Wheatly to Goshen   Florence to Eugene

The more often we are lost the faster the highways

fray to straw   half my face turned brown to music

## ANOTHER EPIPHANY

It was chilly and the dragonfly hung like a leaf

completely as if it was not unusual for an azalea

to make one easily this being

only one example of what it might take for you

to wise up to the marvelous even the everyday

water so loving it whistles on the stove for you

## TRANSPLANTS

Whatever lives in a place already are the gods there: jaguars,

wolves, a *water hummingbird* as Mayans called the kingfisher,

right down to the chair upstairs at the Monet exhibition

for the King of France, sewn in gold bees. Downstairs, Monet

has suggested another bed of iris near the pond, *fleur de lis*,

and Frances herself a corolla from a white blanket wakes up

asking for water. Monet the gardner doesn't match this

even with his caretakers. The whole bedspread her hair

blooms out of is covered with stitched roses, neat as an acre

planted at Creighton Nursery, so every moment around her

is in flower and looked on with pleasure.   Outside, the sun

has gardened between bricks a pale fungus that complements

the paint.   Some windows have sleepy eyes.   Some shades

are partially open, and the ones that are see plastic necklaces

hung in the trees from the old gods that swarmed in February

together with the resident warblers.

## ORNATE

Ornate is being disparaged again

but not by me

My mornings still have their flaming coats

buttoned with sunup

My trees are papered with gold leaf

edges making more moons in daylight

Austerity is something history does

in its guilt-filled Calvinist phases

The crenelated fugues I wrote yesterday

with my pen of Venus Comb Murex

came elaborately into existence like woven brocades

satin anthologies spun out among the galaxies

experience sculpted to lace

## EROSION AND CEZANNE

You know when you look at the page and the space

between the words begins to swim and light up

and suddenly rivers are spilling to the bottom

of the page like Pachinko and its silver bearings

making song or winning by what they hit,

not like talking, like poetry, by whatever you call it

when something makes magnificent sense by unusual

means, a shape under an umbrella that becomes sea:

crab spiders, merry widow, octopus, and the lines of the

hemisphere are like flatboats down Ohio and the Nile,

rain on the window explaining a watershed, the highlights

of the loquacious rivers of the world, the banks going yellow

as you blink in reverie, birthing in blood in the late sunset

afternoon at Mt. San Victoire, erosion, and Cezanne it is said

tore down the hills not just once, once and for all.

## BEFORE THEIR EYES

People in the lobby for breakfast are watching

ducks shot down from a cloud

of their own making above a marsh in Wisconsin

are mentioning their trips and biscuits

their far flung points of origin while the floating bodies

are fetched by black dogs

The dead and the living pass through each other

right before their eyes

their breaths and neutrinos hover a moment

then plummet like teals

## MISSED

The fig came and went with the children

Already it is twenty years

And the pine is five times above them

The missing are missed

The I-beams under the house next door

are shinbones so the whole

can be lifted and removed like memories

leaves re-explaining last year

aromas of the lake's small Johnson's

## FOLLOWING

We had been following spring rivers

traveling between little rooms

with yellow lights and small refrigerators

I had been assembling rivers of my own

out of spare parts none of them water

apples and lacewings   antibodies

on their way to a limited consciousness


Evenings full of sleepers each room

with tics of things settling

the drifting weight of the others   sighing

Saying one thing meaning another   Sleep with me

Despite some uncomfortable reminders

Exits and Emergency Escapes posted on the walls

I followed my words like light from crushed rock

Later I will tell her what I heard of the lost hikers

found praying to whiteness in the high Cascades

## POETRY

No it is not music, but a few

rhythmic similarities you can't escape, as you can't

composition in painting, or slight conversation

that is speech but not *a* speech,

and no need to talk about singing unless a choir

assembles or the Dixie Hummingbirds,

the Mighty Clouds of Joy with lyrics and with notes.

It is evidence of our separate lives together

how mind arises from complexity.

And not heartfelt, heart is too busy with the blood.

And not out loud, except with an ear against you,

but in silence as leaf shadows refocus on the floor

like the bride zero, the thinking

we are working into a sequence of plain surprises,

hap and cry-life, and how close, when successful,

to picking the best horse, the most perfectly conformed,

turned drastic and demanding.

## OPPORTUNITY

The window of opportunity is often

made of that rippled glass for showers

with a screen beyond that and a valley

filled with clouds and fog keeping things from us

It's understandable   We are not lovable

I hear insects counting stars   They have

their own necessities   I know the paths

to understanding are like slug trails

promissory scripts   expectations I touch

with the hand I use for smoothing

## ESCAPE VELOCITY

No more in love than usual but faster than before

each reflection revs up a private life

Sand ruffles underwater like the sheets beneath us

nervously anticipating

the swift and widespread suicide of lights

To judge by the sound of the air conditioner

we are going very fast

Our room travels with the planet the Ramada's

accelerating bedspreads out of breath

## THE FUTURE

Smoke tells it   the jumbled dice bones

of the foot and hand

even the saddleback worm tells winter

even Christina from the Weather Channel

backdropped by clouds

while outside straws and matchsticks are cast

Still these predictions are easier

than retelling the past where even the list

of the missing is missing

## EUCARYOTE

The last of the sea oat panicles

are still lush in November,

but drooping and just 3% fertile.

They engender by their roots.

Whether the shadow empties itself

back into the brass planter tonight

or the oxides drain out the unusables

into gathering greys, I know them both.

I tell my favorite XX and her deep brown eyes

I am thrilled just to be nucleated,

to have ways to say Frances, look

at the iridescent beetles, the xanthic

hills of Connecticut or Maine,

the unusual hyena-fly down on its haunches.

## SWOON

Not the kind where weak with grieving

one voluntarily dissolves in a glass of vodka,

but as if purposely losing balance and falling

into the beckoning designs of a Persian carpet

made of tinted strings, neurons meshed artfully

and apparently in comfort, sinking thankfully

into a swag of ivies, walled gardens indebted

to a privacy of paradise in counterfeit,

or a historic page of calfskin, gold covered

in traceries, an eye seeing or sensing chaos,

a maze, resolving into a man and a shadow

moving together ecstatic and transformed.

## DOMESTICS

Razor wire was the telephone

sharp as fire inside the house

black bread held in the teeth

to keep from tearing

metal drawers clicked shut

overcrowded with knives

outside the window the beautiful

datura hung white with poison

I know there is tragedy here

why are there not more sirens

## MY LUCKY STARS

They are all lucky   my stars   the archer   the fish

actinosphaerium   even if they prove to be wren skeletons

and I count them as numerous as companies

that send me endless gummed labels with my name

But today the sky is too thick and a hundred things

have plowed into it my lucky stars are occluded

I send money for a chart and there they are

The clouds had them moving above like a protractor

My fortunate stars my lucky billions   I lift my glass

and there is the spot I've read about   punty mark

asterisms running out of names and numbers

yet I hear coughs coming from the shuttered room

## PAGEANT

The hour was phosphorus and the dark

went lime and the concrete saints of Portland

decorating the bridge to the river fluttered

and talked among themselves and the bridge

and the lights were individually explained

and something fiddled with the microphones

and the horses lined up in the starting gates

the audience and planets struggled to attend

## PICTURE WINDOW

Below me, asking themselves into the water

but shyly

so as not to intrude, a necklace of larches,

of lindens,

a child's drawing with the rays of the trees

shown inward

resting their bird-filled arms on the reliable

uplift of reflection

They lie down alive   I am recording my heart

It is resting, weightless

I see a future   The window takes my hand

## SOLVE FOR X

x the unknown about which we know nothing,

but suspect: x on the eyes for knocked out,

innocence protected by the x of anonymity

until succession was revived, crossed over

like blood to the lungs and back: x in the heart,

oxygen reddening it, crossroads of the last gasp,

arms over chests an echo, light isosceles twice:

the lungs of morning and afternoon puffing

from traipsing blood through the entanglement

with things: love tied to tumbleweeds, candles

afloat in the unnamed, the slightest touch.

## LOGO

Certainly nothing from Latin. Not for us. Americans.

Maybe a slight variation on *crazy* in Spanish.

And not symmetrical either. A few burned figures in a bass boat

and a sun with palmetto rays up behind like fireworks.

And the morning should add some of its designs: a heart laughing

too fast from last night. Crisp shadows not soft like afternoon's.

In such an arrangement anything could happen.

Out there a man in a Whaler measures his trout on a yardstick.

Twice it didn't reach but finally it goes in a cooler with the Buds

by him jutting its jaw or squeezing or the fish giving up trying

to be smaller.


The object is simple: Come home. Bring back an idea

of wilderness no matter how small and illegal. Include the Blue Angels

maybe one crab female or one fish showing living in the past is still possible.

And there I was hauling the dead limb when down the driveway

a path like memory was the dog I buried years ago as a car-hit pup

now grown turned female and living elsewhere.

We sat down by the water with sure enough a bass boat out there

while I combed out her knots. The usually symbolic and totally impossible were reconciled. First Fourth the beach wasn't littered with rockets.

Frances asked last night why there weren't more blue fireworks.

When it comes to what counts it's always the *and so on* that matters.

Decorations around those involved. Presentments and mottos arched over.

## WATER LONG ENOUGH

I can take you to where the two dogs are buried.

In the overgrowth is a depression

where the happy flesh and last blankets dissolved.

If you hear water long enough, you make out conversations,

see one pine tickling the moon,

see paths on lumber where the lizards crisscrossed,

young oaks handholding and the dead

under us expectantly reaching for each other.

The conversations are old overseas,

like water to the dogs looking back over their shoulders,

waxing and waning like radio, like tides.

## I KNOW ICE

From afar life is zigzagged like a stick in water

you must drink it to know

and what really happened as a child is like a moth trying

to call back the worm

but in the midnight minus luck it can happen

I remember once I fit in a single sink

water was hand-pumped into   A chick from Easter last

came up the woodpile to look in

What became of it other than this picture

an eager beak nodding in its walk I do not know

I know ice was delivered by a horse

and a man with a rubber apron

Before that I was one of the embryo photographs in *LIFE*

a pink sloth backlit so my veins were the blood rivers

in an egg   a delta in a lens

My hands began unfolding like a map on a napkin

isotherms   isostocies   America del Sur

There were War Bonds at the band shell at Lake Harriet

the woman I hoped for who was the name of the lake

Some of the last things I still believe years later

I did not fall in love   I walked   A mosquito ate out of my hand

## ARDOR

A product of their hours and the hours

of those intersected with them

and their intersections with others even smaller

small bones crumbled to make a hand

those gathered to see what the ruins have written

loved like another verb caress

a smoothing to order an admiration more

a soothing from calming the hair to rest

a wearing away arousal a summing up in touch

a longing looking back   cats scattering

## DEFINITION

A noise came and someone said helicopter

but it was a tear really

a tear in the fabric of the sky so it was defined

finally as a cloth

a threadbare night sky dropped over everything

unlighted

though dawn showed how fragile it was

the whole sky

beautifully woven and holding our breaths for us

## HATCHERY

A confinement containing a sense of breaking out.

So few and rare they could start things up again.

Save things a while before releasing so we can believe

in them again and the fabled stories of abundance.

Swallows strafe the channels where they silvered up

below the signs that described their names,

the flashed facts visible above as shapes as shadows,

and below through the windows as endless anticipation,

poignancies of lives amid the heavy machinery of life

lying next to the river where one night a door opens

to the welcoming spillway and history begins.

## LAST WORD

The opposite of clockwork is not chaos

There are no opposites no therefores

Wood crying is the smoke in whisky

Nerves in the neck are the origins of sleep

The flower in the skull is a dumb garden

No one speaks with authority for long

We are connected by nothing we can prove

While we are thinking a thorax hits the glass

This is not the last word on the subject

## ACKNOWLEDGMENTS

*42 Opus*, Don't Forget Us

*Arts & Letters*, Water Long Enough

*Bayou*, Every Day

*The Chattahoochee Review*, The Inevitable*

*Elk River Review*, Centuries to Quit

*Kestrel*, Reminders

*Mid-American Review*, I Know Ice

*Marlboro Review*, Proof

*Memorious*, Following

*Octopus*, Missed; The Future

*Perihelion*, The Usual Horses; You Helpless

*Phoebe*, Logo

*Salamander*, That Close

*Square Lake*, Fear of Fire

*Swink* (online), A Priori

*Tar Wolf*, Transplants

*The Notre Dame Review*, Full; All This Instead

*The Gettysburg Review*, Reminders; Easy Believers; Whether Neither

*The Pedestal*, Ardor

*Terraine.Org*, Precarious **

*The Weary Blues Anthology,* New Binary Press (Ireland), Continental, Solve for X

My thanks to the editors of the magazines in which these poems first appeared, some in different versions. I also wish to acknowledge several people that have shown continuing interest in my work over the years, especially Paul Sweeney, Dale Wisely, and Frances, always. A special thanks goes to David Dodd Lee at Indiana University South Bend for selecting this book, and to Nick Kuder, John-Mark Cuarto and Paul Sizer at The Design Center of Western Michigan University for its design and production.

*\* Selected by Ted Kooser for the American Life in Poetry Series (#159)*
*\*\* Selected for Dzanc Books' Best of the Web anthology*

Allan Peterson is a poet and visual artist whose work has appeared in print and online in national and international journals for many years. He is the author of four books: *Fragile Acts*, McSweeney's Poetry Series, a finalist for both the 2013 National Book Critics Circle Award and the Oregon Book Award; *As Much As*, Salmon Press, Ireland; *All the Lavish in Common*, 2005 Juniper Prize, University of Massachusetts Press; *Anonymous Or*, Defined Providence Prize, and six chapbooks, notably *Omnivore*, winner of the 2009 Boom Prize from Bateau Press, *Any Given Moment*, Right Hand Pointing (online), and *Stars on a Wire*, University of Alabama's Institute for the Book Arts, 1989. His work appears in several anthologies: *American Poetry At the End of the Millennium*, *Poetry of the American Apocalypse*, (*Green Mountains Review*), *Don't Leave Hungry: 50 Years of the Southern Poetry Review*, and in critical essays in Stephen Burt's *Close Calls with Nonsense: Reading New Poetry*. His work appears as #159 in Poetry Laureate Ted Kooser's "American Life in Poetry." He has received prizes from *Alligator Juniper*, *Arts & Letters*, *GSU Review*, *The American Poetry Journal*, *Comstock Review*, among others, and fellowships from the National Endowment for the Arts and The State of Florida. He splits his time between the Pacific Northwest and Northwest Florida.

204